Survival Guide for Teens

A Simple Guide to Self-Discovery, Social Skills, Money Management and All the Most Essential Life Skills You Need to Learn as a Teenager

Emily Carter

acknowledge that the author is not engaged in the rendering of legal, financial, medical or professional advice. The content within this book has been derived from various sources. Please consult a licensed professional before attempting any techniques outlined in this book.

By reading this document, the reader agrees that under no circumstances is the author responsible for any losses, direct or indirect, that are incurred as a result of the use of the information contained within this document, including, but not limited to, errors, omissions, or inaccuracies.

Table of Contents

Your Free Gift

Having the right mindset is the key when it comes to achieving success in any area of your life. As a way of saying thank you for your purchase, I want to offer you my book *Unleashing Your Potential: A Teenager's Guide to Developing a Growth Mindset and Opening Your Path to Success* for completely FREE of charge.

To get instant access, just go to:

https://lifeskillbooks.com/survival-guide-free-bonus

Inside the book, you will discover…

- The difference between a fixed and growth mindset, how your mindset impacts your personal growth and success, and why a growth mindset is the one you should adopt.
- Practical strategies to cultivate a growth mindset, from daily habits to overcoming obstacles.
- How to utilize a growth mindset to supercharge your academic and career success.
- And much more!

But wait, there's more to come…

In addition to the *Unleashing Your Potential* eBook, I want to give you two additional special bonuses…

Bonus 1:

The Essential Summer Job Handbook: The Teen's Guide to a Fun and Profitable Summer

Inside this exciting guide, you will discover…

- The many benefits of having a summertime job, from earning extra cash to gaining valuable experience and skills that will set you up for success in the future.
- The different types of jobs available for teens at different ages, and how to market yourself effectively to potential employers.

- Practical tips for avoiding being taken advantage of, and advice on tax considerations that every working teen needs to know.

Bonus 2:

Raising Teens With Confidence: 10 Exclusive Blog Posts on Parenting Teens

I know this sounds boring if you're a teen, and that's completely fine. But for you parents out there, these unreleased blog posts offer a great opportunity to learn some new effective ways of parenting your teen.

Inside this compilation, you will discover…

- Invaluable insights and practical tips on how to navigate the challenges of parenting teenagers, from setting boundaries and dealing with mood swings to managing serious issues like drink and drug use.
- How to pick your battles wisely and let go of the small stuff, while still maintaining a strong connection with your teen and encouraging them to open up to you.
- Effective strategies for getting your teen to help out more at home, and how to strike the right balance between being a supportive parent and allowing your teen to develop their independence.

If you want to really make a change in your life for the better and get ahead of 95% of other teens, make sure to go to the website below and grab these free books now too.

https://lifeskillbooks.com/survival-guide-free-bonus

Introduction

*It takes courage to grow up and
become who you really are.*

–E.E Cummings

Well done for taking steps to improve yourself. It is great that you are wise enough to know that the work you put into yourself today will pay off. Hard work and effort are never in vain; what you choose to invest in, your life will reflect.

Have an ambitious vision of what and who you want to become, and aim as high as you want because the sky is certainly not the limit. Be grateful, live enthusiastically, learn, grow, inspire, love, and live every moment with intention.

Growing up is scary and exciting, but a journey you must enthusiastically embrace. Your parents, loved ones, friends, or mentors cannot take your life journey for you, and neither can they make good, responsible decisions for you. You control your journey, and decide where you want to go, what you want to do, and how you want to do what you want to do.

Not everyone's journey is the same, and there is no "right" way to "grow up" and navigate life, and you will make mistakes along the way! Throughout life, you will be faced with choices, most of which will not be easy, and at times you will make the wrong choices.

Making the wrong choices doesn't mean that your journey is over or that you are a failure; it means that you have an opportunity for personal development. When you make bad or wrong choices, always dust yourself off and pick yourself up again.

Take one day at a time and strive to do your best in all that you do. Remember that even the most successful people make mistakes, and what makes them stand out is that they do not give up.

Your teen years will be over before you know it. Time goes by quickly and has already gone by quickly. It could feel like only a few years ago when you first started school, and now you are heading toward taking your first steps into adulthood. Brace yourself; in the not-too-distant future, the challenges you face now will be a distant memory.

It is likely frightening to think that very soon, your tie-dye shirts, oversized sweaters, and chunky sneakers will be exchanged for a little more "grown-up" professional-looking clothing. Also, it is nearly time to pack your PlayStation away and go to work. Soon you will be managing your finances and making decisions about where your life is heading.

You will move into your own home, where you will pay regular bills like gas and water; and keep the WIFI connected. Oh, and you will also be responsible for controlling your mental and physical health. Mom and Dad aren't necessarily going to be right there making sure you are looking after yourself.

Life is an adventure that is pretty fast-paced, and keeping up with the never-ending changes can be overwhelming. With phenomenal advancements in technology like Artificial Intelligence, Augmented Reality, Virtual Reality, the Internet of Things (IoT), 5G Networks, and Blockchain, who can tell what the future holds?

The reality is that in life, you cannot really be certain of much. In this day and age, the best you can do is equip yourself with the resources you have. This survival guide will be a valuable resource that you can use to equip yourself for what lies ahead.

I can honestly say my life has been an exciting journey. As a mother of two kids and being married to my high school sweetheart, I understand the challenges that come with trying to balance family and work life.

Spending much of my free time volunteering at a local food bank, I am deeply passionate about helping others. I love spending time outdoors hiking, traveling, and reading personal development books.

Working over 10 years in education and parenting fields, I noticed a gap in education when it comes to teaching essential life skills to teens and young adults. How can anyone expect you as a young person to succeed in life without the proper skills and guidance?

I made a life-changing choice to use my knowledge and write comprehensive guides that cover essential life skills for teens. My hope is that my books will empower you to live your best life and reach your full potential.

In this *Survival Guide for Teens,* we discuss things that really matter. We explore topics like self-discovery and your true identity so that you can find out what makes you who you are. We also look at some important relationship and social skills you need to make sure that you can have healthy relationships.

Next, we will discuss important financial skills that you need so that you can work well with your money. We also explore some practical life skills that will help you prepare for day-to-day life in adulthood. Then we discuss the importance of looking after your physical and mental health so that you can truly make the most of your life. Lastly, we explore one of the most important aspects of your life: education and career.

Let us hop right in and explore self-discovery and your identity, and find out what makes you uniquely you!

Chapter 1: Identity and Self-Discovery

*Knowing yourself is the beginning of
all wisdom.*

–Aristotle

Who are you? Where exactly do you fit in this big, beautiful world? You are most definitely not who the bullies at school said you were; or what your little sister or brother labeled you as. There is also more to what makes you who you are than your favorite clothing, color, or meal.

Think back on the changes that you have already experienced and how far you have come in such a short time. First, you were that cute baby who relied on Mom and Dad for almost everything. Then you went through the toddler stage, where you started exploring the world with your newly found independence.

Next, you ventured into the world without Mom and Dad for the very first time, and you went to school. At school, you made friends, grew even more independent, and began learning all sorts of interesting things. Now you are at a place where you are moving even further away from the safety net that your parents lovingly gave you.

Life is an exciting journey filled with discovery and self-discovery. As you experience different stages of life, you discover, question, and embrace new aspects of your true self. In this chapter, we are going to discuss what makes you, you. We will also have a look at some self-help techniques that you can try to get to know yourself a little better.

As you get to know your authentic self, you shape your life, future career, interests, and goals around things that bring you happiness and that interest you. The more you learn and grow and find out what really motivates you, the more your confidence and sense of worth grow.

What Makes You Uniquely You?

As you start giving some thought to this question, you will realize what makes you and that there are a lot of different things that make up your identity. Firstly, family dynamics play a huge part in who you are. Your parents, siblings, and family traditions all contribute to your sense of self and how you function in the world.

You also have your very own personal style. Your choice of trending clothing, hairstyles, and accessories all help you to express your true identity. As you know, your fashion choices are a fabulous way for you to showcase your uniqueness.

Another thing that makes you fantastically unique and that is part of your identity is your hobbies, passions, and interests. Things like the music you listen to, art, writing, and sports all play a part in making you who you are.

What you personally value also forms part of your unique identity. As you go through life and develop your own set of belief systems, values, and principles, these things shape your identity. This can also include values that are related to social justice, environmentalism, and even equality.

All of your ambitious academic pursuits and career goals also play a major role in developing your sense of purpose and direction in life. Your education path and choice of academic subjects, extracurricular activities, and future aspirations shape your identity.

Your social groups and the fun people you choose to hang out with all influence your identity and give you a sense of belonging as well. For instance, the book club, tennis team, and online communities that you belong to all impact your identity and how you fit into the world.

Another aspect that influences your identity is your cultural background which influences things like the language you speak, your customs, and your celebrations. Your cultural heritage, traditions, and values all play a massive role in shaping your identity.

Your unique personal experiences also play a huge role in who you are and contribute to your personal growth and perspective. Unique experiences like travel, volunteering, or overcoming challenges all shape who you are.

Self-Discovery Exercises

For your happiness and well-being, it is important that you never stop working on self-discovery. As you go through life, so many aspects of your identity change. With self-awareness, you can live a life that is in line with your core values and authentic self.

Choose not to be like so many others who work hard toward achieving their goals but do not put enough effort into self-discovery. Not knowing your worth or values can leave you leading an unfulfilling life. Always know your worth, your core values, and what makes you, you!

If you are struggling to get in touch with your authentic self, various self-discovery exercises can help you. If one self-discovery exercise does not work for you, do not give up; try another one. It is important that you realize that self-discovery is a very personal journey that only you can embark on.

Here are some empowering self-discovery exercises that you can use to help you to explore your unique identity.

Journaling

Firstly, you can give journaling a try. Journaling can help you to express your thoughts, feelings, and experiences in a healthy way. Make a habit of journaling every day, where you spend time reflecting on your day, writing about your dreams and aspirations, and exploring your emotions.

Mindfulness and Meditation

Another awesome self-discovery tool is mindfulness and meditation practices. Take some time each day to explore different mindfulness techniques and meditation practices to help you become more self-aware and present in the moment. Techniques that you could try include things like deep breathing exercises, body scans, or guided meditations.

Vision Boards

Create a vision board by collecting inspiring images, words, and symbols that represent your unique goals, dreams, and aspirations. This creative visual representation can help you gain clarity about your deepest desires and aspirations.

Express Yourself

Tap into your emotions and gain deep insight into who you really are by expressing yourself creatively. Take some time out to do art, listen to or even create music or write. Creative expression is one of the most empowering forms of self-discovery, so choose a creative outlet that allows you to be yourself and express yourself.

Strengths and Values Assessment

Use the internet to find some online strengths and values assessments or reflection exercises. There are many online assessments and exercises that can help you to identify your strengths, qualities, and values. You can also look for questionnaires or reflection prompts that encourage self-exploration. These can include questions about your true passions, fears, values, and what you envision for your future.

Role Models

Spend time researching and learning about people who inspire you. These role models and inspirational figures can be anyone from your favorite film star, talk show host, historical figure, artist, or athlete. Choose anyone who has really amazing qualities that you admire and that inspire you to do great things. Then take some time to think about why these people inspire you; this can really help you to understand your own values and aspirations better.

Time in Nature

There is nothing like spending time in nature or outdoors to help you connect with yourself on a far deeper level. Being out in natural surroundings can give you a sense of peace that can help you to reflect on all the things in your life.

Remember that self-discovery is ongoing, and there is no right or wrong way to go about it. Always be open to new and exciting experiences, and reach out for help if you need any. Feedback from supportive people can be a great tool for self-discovery, as can seeking therapy from professionals who are trained to help others discover themselves.

In the next chapter, we are going to have a look at why it is important for you to have good relationship and social skills. We will explore different kinds of social skills and relationships that you will have. You will also be given valuable tips on how you can improve your social skills and build healthy relationships.

Chapter 2: Relationships and Social Skills

The future belongs to those who learn more skills and combine them in creative ways.

–Robert Greene

A great support system, extraordinary experiences, and creating memories are all part of what makes life enjoyable. Not many things can bring you as much happiness as spending fun times with others.

In this chapter, we will discuss relationships and social skills, why they are important, and things you can do to improve these skills. We will also briefly cover the relationships you must work on during this essential time.

When you feel loved, valued, and supported, you can take on challenges and are inspired to embark on adventures. The healthier your relationships are, the healthier you will be, and the more you will radiate self-confidence.

Relationships give you opportunities, and the more you interact with others, the more you learn and grow. Your relationships help you to gain new interesting perspectives, develop empathy and valuable life skills. Trust, communication, and conflict resolution are all important skills you need in your relationships.

Remember that being around positive people who uplift and support helps you pursue your goals and dreams. Healthy relationships can inspire you and give you a sense of accountability to be your best. Think about how many days you would have gone without making your bed in the morning if it was not for Mom motivating and teaching you accountability.

During difficult times, it is your relationships that can offer you comfort and help you manage your stress better. Meaningful relationships help you feel connected to something bigger than yourself and help you feel accepted, understood, valued, and like you belong.

Types of Relationships

The sense of belonging a community provides—whether it's a neighborhood, religious group, or cultural organization—is different from that of a family. That first really important relationship you have, and where you feel you belong, is with your family. Usually, these are the people that shower you with unconditional love, support, and guidance.

Family relationships can be close or distant and are not all the same, as there can be different levels of emotional connection. Your emotional bond with your mom or dad may differ from that you have with an aunt or uncle, for instance.

Next are friendships, which can be casual or close. You probably made your first friend in kindergarten or at a playdate. When you have similar interests, values, and experiences, your friends can give you companionship, support, and social opportunities.

You will also form relationships with school staff like teachers, counselors, mentors, coaches, and extracurricular leaders. When you need it, healthy relationships with teachers and mentors can offer you guidance, encouragement, and support in your academic and personal development. Involvement in sports teams, clubs, or other extracurricular activities also helps you to create relationships that provide guidance and mentorship.

Throughout life, you will also encounter acquaintances, which are casual relationships. An acquaintance could be someone who lives in your street, the lady working at the local store, or a bus driver. While you may not form close relationships with acquaintances, they are still part of your world.

Online relationships are another type of relationship you are likely to form. You might form these relationships online on social media, in study groups, forums, gaming communities, and video chats.

While online relationships can give you extra support and a sense of community, be cautious of who you befriend online, you do not always know who is on the other side of the screen. Always be mindful of your digital etiquette and use social media platforms responsibly and respectfully.

Another relationship you are bound to have is romantic, which will give you a special emotional connection, intimacy, and personal growth. Romantic relationships can be exciting, rewarding, challenging, and complicated. Usually characterized by butterflies and oxytocin releases, these are intimate relationships among people with special connections.

Next, as you start your career, you will build relationships with your colleagues. These relationships can either be formal or informal and will involve different levels of teamwork. For any type of relationship that you encounter, you will need certain skills to build and navigate these different relationships. Let's look at a few important relationship and social skills you will need.

Relationship and Social Skills

Healthy relationships do not just magically appear; they take effort and can become lifelong friendships. Healthy relationships need to be nurtured, meaning you must show kindness, appreciation, and understanding to others.

Authenticity

Authenticity is key in relationships and life. Choose to shine and show the world the real you, not the person you think the world will love. Embrace your true self and surround yourself with people who accept and appreciate you for who you are.

Empathy

Empathy is another skill that you need to develop so that you can enjoy healthy relationships. When you can develop genuine empathy and understanding for others, you can understand and relate to the feelings and experiences of others. If you empathize with others, you can see things from their unique perspective and show compassion.

Communication

To have happy relationships, you also need to be able to communicate openly and honestly so that you avoid unwanted misunderstandings. Learning to express yourself well and listening well are important skills to make your relationships with others happy.

Conflict Resolution

Even healthy relationships are not all peaches and cream. There will be times when conflict and disagreements arise; the trick is to learn how to resolve conflict healthily. Healthy conflict resolution involves active listening and finding win-win solutions.

Boundaries

The secret ingredient to healthy relationships; boundaries. Having boundaries protects your space, time, things, energy, and those of others. Knowing and respecting your own and others' boundaries is essential. Always communicate your boundaries clearly and, at the same time, be mindful of the boundaries of others.

Quality Over Quantity

It is not about how many friends you have but rather the quality of those relationships. Who wants to surround themselves with people who don't bring them some measure of joy? Focus on genuine connections with people who support and uplift you; it's not about the numbers.

Embrace Diversity

Respect, embrace, and celebrate diversity. Expanding your social circle involves going out and meeting new people. Choose to be a person who learns from people with different backgrounds, cultures, and perspectives. Respect and value the differences that make each person on this planet unique.

Mixing with people with different perspectives, backgrounds, and cultures will expand your worldview. When you better understand the world, you broaden your horizons, and this will help you to become more open-minded.

Social Media

Using social media, you can connect and form relationships with interesting people, but remember that it is not a measure of your self-worth. Social media lets people show the world a version of themselves that they want to portray, so do not compare yourself to others based on their online persona. Use social media mindfully and always prioritize real-life relationships and connections.

Self-Care

Remember self-care when developing relationships, online or in real life. Make time to take care of your well-being to recharge and rejuvenate yourself. When you are not doing well physically or mentally, this can impact your relationships, so practice self-care. Self-care activities can include meditation, journaling, or spending time in nature. Remember that the more you invest in yourself and your relationships, the more rewarding your life will be.

Tips to Develop Relationship and Social Skills

Your relationships impact your emotional well-being, personal growth, and happiness. So how exactly can you improve your relationship and social skills?

Listen

Start by practicing active listening. Communicating with others means paying attention to what they say, maintaining eye contact, and showing genuine interest.

Join Clubs and Organizations

Improve your relationship and social skills by joining clubs or organizations to participate in activities you are interested in, meet new people, and connect with others.

Volunteer

When you step out of your comfort zone and do some volunteer work, you can meet and interact with different people and develop empathy. Volunteering gives you an opportunity to do good in society and develop relationships and social skills. If volunteering really is not your thing, try participating in team sports, group projects, or collaborative activities to develop your skills.

Ask Others

The people who know you best can give you valuable feedback about how they feel you communicate and interact with others. You can use this feedback to improve your relationship and social skills. If you struggle with self-confidence, you can role-play with a close friend or family member to help you build confidence and improve your problem-solving skills.

Self-Reflection, Self-awareness, and Emotional intelligence

Be mindful, reflect on your behavior and interactions with others, and work on areas that need improvement. Remember to be assertive and always express your thoughts, opinions, and needs respectfully and confidently.

Work on developing your self-awareness and emotional intelligence skills so that you can recognize and manage your emotions and the emotions of others. Always analyze situations, identify solutions, and make informed decisions.

Look up to people with strong relationships and social skills and learn from them. Developing social skills takes time and practice, so be kind to yourself and celebrate your progress! Be adaptable, open-minded, and willing to consider different perspectives.

Remember that time management skills give you enough time for your responsibilities and fun. You only live once, so set goals and believe in yourself. In the next chapter, we are going to explore finances. Yes, money is that thing that makes the world go round and that you need to work wisely with.

Chapter 3: Financial Literacy

A penny saved is a penny earned.

–Benjamin Franklin

How exciting is it to start saving toward your future goals? You are probably already imagining what driving a brand-new Soul Red Crystal Metallic Mazda CX-5 will feel like! The chances are good that you are also thinking about how cool your clothes will be when you get everything you like.

But, oops, slow down there for a moment; let's not forget those bills you will have to pay. Feels a bit overwhelming, right? Don't panic because you are the master of your financial destiny and can create your own reality.

When it comes to managing your finances, you can't let your money disappear like socks in the laundry. Instead, choose to be wise with your money. To start off, consider saving money in a special piggy bank or an actual banking account, and be disciplined enough not to spend your savings.

Be wise and think twice before saying yes to concert tickets or trendy gadgets that catch your eye. Being financially responsible is like having a trustworthy companion who always backs you up when you're tempted to stray. Remember to follow the golden rule of saving well today so that you can indulge tomorrow.

Learning to work with money is an essential skill you will use for the rest of your life! Even though Mom and Dad might make managing money seem easy, they also had to learn how to manage money to live comfortably. Mom's budgeting skills did not fall out of the heavens; she also bumped her head a few times when she overspent.

Finances Matter

Knowing how to work with money does not come naturally; it is a learned skill developed over time with trial and error. It's never too early or too late to learn how to work with money, and you should aim to establish positive financial habits.

While some say money does not buy happiness, that is not entirely true. Money may not be able to solve all life's problems, but it can bring a measure of opportunity, security, fun, comfort, and happiness.

Expanding your horizons and mastering the art of budgeting, investing, and saving money can help pave the way for your future success. Knowing how to handle your money and bills is important so you can be financially healthy.

When you cannot work with money well, you will struggle, and the quality of your life will suffer. You will also battle to set and achieve financial goals that can help you to build a more secure financial future. However, improving your financial literacy skills means that you are choosing a different path than those who desperately struggle to manage their money.

Basic Financial Concepts

Budgeting is important for managing money and basically means deciding how to spend and save your money. With a budget in place that you are responsible enough to stick to, you can better manage the money that you do have and avoid reckless overspending.

To budget well, you must track your income and expenses and set financial goals. This means watching your money flow and using it wisely. Before spending your money, remember to always look at the bigger picture and prepare for difficult times by saving for a rainy day.

You may have wants like owning your own home one day or buying a new high-tech laptop one day. Unfortunately, at the moment, these things cost way more than you can afford. However, the good news is that saving money can make your future dreams a reality.

For many, saving can be incredibly challenging as they cannot seem to distinguish between needs and wants. Instead of spending money only on their essential needs, they indulge in all their short-term wants and forget to save or invest their hard-earned money.

Investing is fantastic as it can help you grow your wealth over time, but it also involves risk and requires careful research and planning. For some, investing is a little over their heads because they have not invested enough time into researching and planning.

Investing means using your money to earn a return in the future. This can be done by investing in various different things like stocks, bonds, or even real estate.

Just like you would build a luxurious home one brick at a time, remember that wealth is also built similarly. By investing, saving, and implementing other financial strategies, in time, you really can build your net worth. Building wealth also involves managing debt effectively, minimizing taxes, and making intelligent financial decisions that align with your long-term goals.

Credit is another useful financial tool that can be a lifeline in times of need. However, it can also lead to trouble if not managed correctly. With credit, you can easily borrow money through a credit card or loan for purchases you can't afford outright. Understanding credit is important so that you can manage your debt, build your credit history, and maintain a good credit score.

When you start working, it is not as simple as money coming in and going out on the things you want to spend money on. As an "adult," you must pay government taxes. Taxes are the fees you and others must pay to support government programs and services. It is very important that you understand how taxes work and how to file your taxes correctly to avoid penalties and also to maximize your tax benefits.

More Advanced Financial Topics

Once you understand basic financial concepts like budgeting, saving, and investing, exploring more advanced financial topics will only benefit you. While financial topics may seem overwhelming, they are worth becoming familiar with.

It is important that you rule your money and not allow your money to rule you. Do not become a prisoner of money; instead, become the master of your money. Here are some examples of slightly more advanced and involved financial topics that you should take some time to look into:

Credit Scores

A credit score is important and represents your overall creditworthiness or how likely you are to repay debt. You can get loans and credit cards at a good interest rate when you have a good credit score. But if your credit score is bad, it can be hard to get approved, and you might end up paying high-interest rates. Understanding exactly how credit scores work and how you can improve your credit score can help you build a strong credit history and access credit when needed.

Retirement Planning

While no one wants to get old, you do. Before you know it, you will be looking back on the days when you never knew how to create a budget while getting ready to retire. Retirement planning is super important as it involves creating a plan for supporting yourself financially in retirement. This can include saving for retirement through a 401(k) or IRA, estimating your retirement expenses, and creating a plan for how you will withdraw money from your retirement accounts.

Tax Planning

Tax laws can be complicated and can vary from location to location. Tax planning involved minimizing your tax liability through strategies like:

- maximizing your deductions

- taking advantage of tax-advantaged accounts

- timing your income to minimize your tax bill

- timing your expenses to minimize your tax bill

When it comes to taxes, it is important to start from the basics and work your way from there. Become familiar with your tax obligations and keep track of your income. If you are struggling to understand taxes, seek help from a trusted adult, a tax professional, or look for online resources.

Risk Management

Many are clueless when it comes to risk management. Risk management involves protecting yourself and your assets from any unexpected events, like accidents, illnesses, or natural disasters. This can include purchasing insurance, creating an emergency fund, and diversifying your investments.

Business Finance

If you want to own a business, it's important to understand business finance. This will help you manage money, make smart investments, and plan for growth. You should learn about things like financial statements, debt management, and creating good business plans.

Remember that learning about money is ongoing; there is always more to learn. By exploring financial topics, you can become more knowledgeable and make smarter decisions with your money. Knowledge is power, and a strong financial foundation can benefit you.

In the next chapter, we will look at some practical life skills to help you keep on the right path to future success.

Chapter 4: Practical Life Skills

*Of all the life skills available to us,
communication is perhaps the most
empowering.*

–Bret Morrison

Mom and Dad keep the house in one piece and functioning well, look after themselves, you, and your siblings, and still work and have time to do things they love. Although your parents may seem like real-life superheroes, practical life skills are the things that help them to manage life so well.

Life skills are those special skills everyone needs to thrive through everyday life, challenges, and opportunities. Without life skills, a day would be overwhelming and feel nearly impossible to get through.

As you enter adulthood, you'll discover a newfound sense of independence that can be exhilarating yet intimidating and comes with great responsibility. Without practical life skills, navigating life and managing your independence will be far more challenging than it needs to be.

In this chapter, we will look at some practical life skills that you need to be a superhero in your own life. We will explore skills like time management, organizational skills, healthy habit forming, cooking, and cleaning, all seemingly small things that make thriving through life possible. Let's start by looking at some good habits and routines that you can form to help you navigate your newly found independence.

Habits and Routines

By now, you know the value of waking up early, making your bed, and starting your day on a positive note. These are all healthy habits and routines that greatly impact the quality of your life. The good news is that if, up until now, you have not had good habits and routines, there is no time like the present to start making positive changes.

Investing time in developing good habits and routines can put you on the right path to accomplishing your goals and leading a fulfilling, productive life. When trying to form new healthy habits, start by making small everyday changes. Remember that there is no sense in trying to climb a huge mountain when you can barely walk up a steep hill.

Creating Habits Smartly

Developing positive habits and routines takes time and effort, but the rewards that come with them are well worth it. Begin by focusing on one or two small habits or routines at a time that you want to develop. When you are working toward achieving your goals, it's important to break things down into smaller, more manageable steps.

Focus on setting achievable, specific, and measurable goals as you work on developing your new habits or routines. To make sure that you achieve your goals, create a clear plan that includes the following:

- creating a schedule

- identifying any obstacles

- tracking your progress

It is important to keep to your schedule and plan, even during challenging or inconvenient times. While it is not always easy, commitment and consistency will lead to your ultimate success in achieving your goals. You must also be accountable for your actions while working toward healthy and positive habits.

Keeping a record of your progress can inspire you, especially when you take some time to look back and see how far you really have come. Sharing your dreams and ambitions with your loved ones can also keep you committed to achieving your goals. Be sure to acknowledge and celebrate each small achievement along the way, as this will fuel and motivate you to keep striving forward.

Essential Life Skills

Remain focused on building some essential life skills so that you can achieve all that you want to and thrive in life. Some of the most basic life skills that you should focus on developing are:

- time management

- cooking

- cleaning

- organization

Time Management Skills

Time is precious, but it goes by so quickly. It is important that you use the time that you have on your hands wisely. The reality is that without good time management skills, you will find it very difficult to lead a balanced, happy, and successful life.

Many people struggle in different aspects of their lives because they can't seem to get their heads around working well with the time that they have. When you are able to manage your time well, you can better manage your schedule, balance priorities, and unlock your full potential to succeed. Be inspired, and remember that with dedication and self-discipline, you can become a true time management pro!

Cooking

Cooking is a life skill that everyone needs and that you will use for the rest of your life. Being able to cook does not mean that you need to prepare a meal that matches the standards of Gordon Ramsay, but you should be able to prepare meals and understand basic nutrition. When you understand nutrition, you can set up healthy eating plans, go grocery shopping, and work safely with food.

Cleaning

To avoid living in a dirty, unhygienic environment, you have to clean. Cleaning does not mean only washing the dishes; it involves maintaining a dust-free, uncluttered, clean, and organized living environment and includes doing chores like cleaning floors, windows, bathrooms, and your kitchen. Additionally, if you plan on having cute pets in your home, you are going to have to clean up after them too.

Organization

When you have good organizational skills managing your time, space, and things become far easier. Just think about how difficult it is to find your favorite sweater when your wardrobe is disorganized. Being organized means keeping your space tidy, having a system for sorting things, and even using a planner or calendar to remember important tasks and appointments.

By putting effort into developing these basic life skills, you will slowly but surely become more independent, self-sufficient, and confident in navigating the challenges and opportunities that come your way.

Advanced Life Skills

Life skills help you become more resilient, handle challenging situations, make good choices, control your emotions, and communicate well. A strong set of life skills help you control yourself and situations when needed, recover from crises and adapt to changes. These skills can help you succeed in many different areas of your life, including school, work, and relationships.

It is also important to put effort into developing some more advanced life skills like:

- emotional intelligence

- entrepreneurial skills

- leadership skills

- problem-solving

Emotional Intelligence

As briefly mentioned in Chapter 2, being emotionally intelligent means that you can regulate and understand your emotions well. Emotional intelligence also means being able to understand other people's emotions. When you are emotionally intelligent, you are self-aware; empathetic and have also developed your relationship management skills. Additionally, being emotionally intelligent means you are more able to build healthy relationships and handle stress.

Entrepreneurial Skills

Most people think that owning their own business is a walk in the park, but in reality, it requires hard work, focus, and dedication. If you hope to own your own business one day, you will need to develop some essential entrepreneurial skills. However, please note that these skills can also be useful to you if you are not an aspiring entrepreneur. These skills include learning how to identify opportunities, establishing sound business plans, advertising what you have to offer, and managing business finances.

Leadership Skills

While some people are born with natural leadership qualities, others need to work extra hard at developing those abilities. Leading well is essential in many areas of life, for example, if you have hopes to go into business, politics, and even social activism. Good leadership skills make it easier to motivate and direct others toward achieving a common goal. To be a really good leader, you need a few different skills like communication, delegation, and even conflict resolution.

Problem-Solving

Problems are inevitable in life; therefore, knowing how to solve problems is something you need to be able to do. To solve problems well, you must be able to look at situations, be creative and work alone or with others to find the very best answers or solutions. With good problem-solving skills, you can manage difficult situations in your life easier.

Remember that, throughout life, you will be learning and growing, and there will always be more for you to uncover and explore. In the next chapter, we will explore how important it is to look after yourself on all levels. You need to look after your physical and mental health to achieve all that you can.

Chapter 5: Physical and Mental Health

*Slow, deep breathing is important…
It's like an anchor in the midst of an
emotional storm: the anchor won't get
rid of the storm, but it will hold you
steady until it passes.*

–Russ Harris

Be wise and take care of your health so that you can get the most out of life. Sadly, many people do not realize how valuable their health is until it's too late. While it is easy for you to take a walk or a run right now, if you do not look after your physical health, your body will eventually start giving you trouble.

As most people age, they become less physically active, which is concerning given how important good health is to your overall well-being. Your energy levels, motivation, ability to handle setbacks, relationships, and self-confidence are all affected by your physical and mental health.

Without good physical health, your body will not function at its best. From here on out, your ultimate goal should be to look after yourself and keep your body functioning well. So instead of spending time on the couch or on social media, take a walk or a run and get your body moving.

Just as your physical health is essential to your overall well-being, so is your mental health, and you should do everything in your power to take care of it. Not many people realize it, but factors like genetics, environment, and experiences all impact mental health. This chapter will look at some basic health concepts, mental health management, and stress strategies that can help you live your best life.

Basic Health Concepts

Basic health concepts play a major part in laying the foundations for a healthier and happier future. Your teenage years are a significant time of your life where you undergo many mental, physical, emotional, and social changes. It is important for you not only to understand but also embrace basic health concepts so that you can maintain and improve your overall well-being.

Nutrition

Good nutrition is something that many people neglect. Eating well doesn't mean stopping at McDonald's for a burger and fries, a healthy diet should include foods from all the food groups.

Often people fall into the trap of turning to quick and convenient meals so that they can rush back to their busy schedules. However, by eating a balanced diet rich in fruit, vegetables, whole grains, and lean proteins, you look after your body and mind better.

Various health issues and unwanted weight gain result from consuming too much sugar, processed foods, and unhealthy fats. Treat your body with the love and care it deserves by eating a healthy, nutritious diet.

Physical Activity

Regular exercise is good for controlling your body weight and drastically improves your strength, endurance, and mood. The trick to forming and maintaining a regular exercise program is finding and doing activities that you really enjoy, like swimming, biking, dancing, or even team sports. When you make physical exercise enjoyable, it is far easier to build and maintain long-term fitness habits.

Sleep

Despite popular belief, browsing through social media and watching movies is not more important than sleep. While many think sleep is overrated, your body and mind need 8–10 hours of sleep every night to keep healthy. Getting enough sleep helps you stay energized and focused and also helps reduce your risk of physical and mental health problems.

Support System

Life can be stressful at times, and your mental health should always be a priority! It is normal that there will be times when academic pressures, relationships, and personal struggles become overwhelming, and having a good support system can help you through those challenging times. Your friends, family, or even professionals can be your soft place to turn when you feel like you are not coping well with life.

Safe Sex

Yes, your hormones might be all over the place right now, but practicing safe and responsible sexual behavior is crucial. Learn about contraception, sexually transmitted infections (STIs), and consent so that you can make informed decisions about sex and stay healthy. Open and honest communication with your partner and using protection methods, like condoms, can prevent unwanted pregnancies and lower your risk of STIs.

Say "No" To Alcohol and Drugs

Life is not one big party. Educate yourself on the risks associated with alcohol and drug use to make responsible choices. Alcohol and drugs are not cool and not worth experimenting with. While you might think you are just messing about, your choices can potentially destroy your entire life and impact your physical and mental health. Learn about the risks and dangers of substance abuse and make well-informed decisions before you make choices that can change your life forever.

Hygiene

Personal hygiene is important for both your physical and mental health. Wash your hands, take showers, brush your teeth, and wear clean clothes. Put your best foot forward every day and look presentable. Good hygiene helps you feel confident and shows respect for yourself and others.

Stay Informed

Keep up to date about important health topics like vaccinations and screen time so that you can make intelligent choices about your well-being. Remember that taking the time to prioritize your health will help you to reach your full potential.

While stress is a normal part of life, chronic stress negatively impacts both your physical and mental health. It is important to find effective stress management techniques that work for you that you can incorporate into your lifestyle.

Mental Health and Stress Management

People from all walks of life are talking up about their mental health struggles, highlighting just how many people face challenges. There is no shame in admitting that you are not coping well and are struggling with your mental health. The great news is that there are ways for you to manage your mental health troubles and stress better.

Connect

Focusing on connecting and maintaining healthy social connections with friends, family, and supportive people is essential to improve and manage your overall mental health. Take the time to have more uplifting and meaningful conversations and spend one-on-one time with interesting people.

Limit Screen Time

While it is difficult to take a break from TikTok and Facebook, limiting your screen time, especially on social media, can significantly improve your mental health. Start setting healthy boundaries and allocating time for activities that don't involve screens, like reading, exercising, meditation, or spending time outdoors.

Seek Support

Through the struggles of others, we can learn a great deal. If you are struggling with your mental health or stress overload, remember you are never alone. There is always help and hope, whether you talk to a friend or a family member you trust, a mental health professional, or join a support group. Remember that seeking help is a sign of remarkable strength, not weakness. Everyone's journey in life is unique and deeply personal, so find coping strategies that work for you.

Be Grateful

Gratitude in life goes a long way. Start cultivating a gratitude mindset by always acknowledging and appreciating the positive things in your life. Doing this can help shift your focus toward the good things in your life and improve your overall well-being.

Choosing to look after your physical and mental health improves your well-being, happiness, and ability to achieve your goals. Remember that small changes really can make a big difference, and it's never too late to prioritize your health. Looking after your physical and mental health is an ongoing process, and there is always more to learn and explore.

In the next chapter, we will discuss education and career. Just like your personal journey should be tailor-made to fit your unique personality and needs, and so should your career choices. Your career will be a huge part of your life and should be given the attention it deserves.

Chapter 6: Education and Career

*Education is the most powerful
weapon you can use to change the
world.*

–Nelson Mandela

Having a good education makes life easier. Education is a key that will open doors to amazing experiences in your life. Being genuinely committed to your education will give you a chance at some of the most incredible opportunities in life. For example, you can explore exciting career options and apply to more prestigious schools and highly sought-after jobs.

When you focus and invest time and effort into your education, you enhance your critical thinking abilities, expand your knowledge, and broaden your perspectives. With this knowledge and skill set, you can pursue career paths that align with your passions and interests.

If you choose a really satisfying career path that gives you a sense of purpose, one day, you will enjoy financial stability and feel as though you have accomplished something really meaningful in life. Once you have decided on a career, be 100% committed, focus on your education, and work hard to reach your dreams.

In this chapter, we will look at some key career concepts that can help you get working toward your dreams. We also discuss how you can gain "work" experience before entering the working world and explore tips to help you succeed in your future workplace.

Going to Battle

Preparing for your education and career is very much like preparing for war; it takes strategy, knowledge, and skills development. To win in this war, you must recognize your strengths and weaknesses and use them to your advantage.

Are you skilled in math and numbers or more interested in literature? Once you know your academic strengths, work toward improving them. Use any resources you can to improve your natural abilities and develop your mind, like textbooks, online courses, and mentors.

Once you have finally managed to get to graduation day, don't let the cap's weight overshadow your success. Instead, see that cap as a symbol of all the time, dedication, and hard work you put in the classrooms and lecture halls. Remember, a skilled warrior always overcomes and conquers.

Career Concepts

Considering that the average adult works around 45 hours per week, you most certainly do not want to choose a career path you absolutely hate. Imagine dragging yourself off day in and day out that is not fulfilling. Not a pleasant thought, is it?

At first, learning important career concepts may seem confusing, but knowing them can prevent you from getting stuck in an unsatisfying dead-end job. Goal setting, networking, and resume-building are all important career concepts that can help you achieve your dreams.

Write it Down

How would you like your life to look 10 years from now? Identify your future career aspirations and create a plan for achieving your goals. Remember that writing down your plan on paper makes it a little easier to stay focused and motivated.

While you may face obstacles, regularly review your progress and let nothing stop you from achieving your goals. Put your mind in success mode and adjust your goals a little during challenging times if you go off track a little.

Networking for Career Success

As you modify your goals, change your social circle as well. There is most certainly no harm in making your circle a little bigger! Remember that it's not all just about academics; relationships are also important.

Step outside your comfort zone and attend events with like-minded people and explore exciting new opportunities. Networking lets you showcase your personality and make friends who can support and encourage you. By networking with different people, you will learn about different job opportunities, gain insights into industries you are interested in, and connect with potential mentors and collaborators.

Social media can also be a tool you can use to your advantage, especially when you want to network with professional organizations, industry events, and informational interviews. You must also keep your social media accounts looking as decent as possible.

Be wise and use your social media to your advantage by posting things that align with your career of choice. Avoid posting content that could scare a future employer or investor away. Remember that just as new products are marketed with branding, you must also promote and present yourself well.

Resume Building

Resume-building is an essential career concept. You will need to submit a resume for any job that you apply for. Your resume is a document that highlights your skills, experience, and achievements to potential employers. Keep in mind that a strong resume should be tailored to the specific job that you are applying for. Always use clear and concise language, and showcase the things about you that make you shine.

You can also show your eagerness for the job by including a cover letter explaining why you feel you are a good fit and how your skills and experience align with your future employer's needs. Always put your best foot forward and focus on creating an attractive resume.

Gaining Experience

It is almost time for you to try to take on the world and make your unique mark in the workplace. While this is all super exciting, do not jump into the deep end without serious prep work. Buckle up because there is some work you need to do to prepare yourself for the workplace!

Before jumping into the corporate world, you can gain valuable experience in some innovative ways. Never underestimate the power of volunteer work. Not only will volunteering make you feel warm and fuzzy inside, but it will also show future employers that you are a passionate person who is willing to go above and beyond.

Getting an internship is another great way for you to gain practical experience and, at the same time, apply your theoretical knowledge. An internship is really a fantastic way for you to enhance your resume and learn new things.

Actively seek internships and volunteer opportunities in your area that align with your future career goals and interests. Remember that internships and volunteer work can give you valuable experience to help you build your skills and network.

Workplace Success

To lead a really fulfilling life, you need a healthy work-life balance. Achieving a healthy balance between your personal and work life may be difficult, but it's possible. When deciding on a career, always factor in work-life balance and your personal needs.

As you enter the working world, be bold and take on new challenges and responsibilities at work. Work hard on developing new skills and demonstrate your true value to your employer. Never be late for work unless you have a legitimate emergency. If you have an emergency, ensure your employer or supervisor knows you won't be able to come to work on time.

Ask your supervisor or colleagues for feedback on how they feel you are performing and coping at work. Do not be shy; ask for advice on how and in what areas they feel you can improve. Feedback from other people can help you to identify areas for growth and development, and remember to use any criticism you get as an opportunity for personal growth.

Be friendly, professional, and collaborative; always seek opportunities to support and help others at work. Building positive relationships with your colleagues and supervisors can help you succeed. However, remember that your colleagues are not your best friends and that work is not where you should be messing around.

Always be willing to work hard, learn and develop yourself. Stay informed about the latest trends and progress in your field. Always look for opportunities to learn new skills and gain knowledge of new technologies, as this can really help you to stay competitive and advance in your career.

Choose to be a person who thinks outside of the box. Take the initiative and look for ways in which workplace processes can be improved or problems can be solved. Being proactive can showcase your true worth to your employer and set you apart as an engaged and committed employee. To succeed in your workplace, always be committed to your work and go the extra mile. Keep your goals in mind, take initiative, and always strive to do your best.

55

Conclusion

Keep true to the dreams of your youth.

–Friedrich Schiller

Transitioning from childhood to adulthood is exciting; grab hold of opportunities, try new things, and discover your passions. Embrace each new day with great enthusiasm. Learn, grow, smile, and shine. You only have one life, so live it well and view each day as a chance to grow, achieve goals, keep your mind active, and explore new things.

View each day as an opportunity to take care of yourself and your loved ones. Share your happiness with others and spread positivity wherever you go. Shine brightly and light up the world with your uniqueness.

In this *Survival Guide for Teens*, topics were covered, and tips were given to help prepare you for life. This book highlighted the importance of self-discovery and identity and looked closely at what makes you, you. You were also given tips on how you can truly discover the real you.

Your teenage years are exciting and filled with self-discovery and growth. Enjoy your journey and be fabulous. Embrace your individuality and unique qualities. Remember that the people who cannot accept and love you for who you are don't need a seat in the front row of your life.

This book also explored the importance of healthy relationships and gave tips on developing your relationship and social skills. Do not let people suck you dry and steal your joy. Celebrate your strengths and interests, and don't conform to society's expectations.

Spend time with people who inspire you to be your best. Remember that being around supportive and uplifting people will improve your happiness and well-being. Spend time listening to motivational speakers and follow any good advice that you are given. Set your standards and expectations as high as you want to, and don't settle for mediocrity; live large! Be bold and associate with people already at a place where you dream of being.

Financial literacy and the importance of being able to work wisely with money was also covered in this book. We discussed some important aspects of finances, like budgeting, saving, taxes, and planning for your future so that you can live a financially healthy life.

We also explored various practical life skills like cooking, cleaning, organizing, and time management. Time goes by quicker than you realize, so spend your time wisely and use the practical life skills you have learned in this book to achieve your dreams. Also, explore more practical life skills so that you can equip yourself to live life well.

This book also explained the importance of looking after your physical and mental health. Remember that you only have one mind, body, and soul, so treasure them. While you may be tempted to skip self-care, remember that doing so will impact your well-being. Get enough sleep, eat nutritious food, exercise regularly, and engage in activities that really bring you real joy.

Lastly, we covered education and career, where we explored some career concepts that can help you make long-term career choices that are right for you. Do not overlook the value of a good education; stay focused and fill your mind with the knowledge that can help you achieve your dreams.

Don't be a person who realizes later on in life that they spent way too much time doing things that they were not passionate about. Embrace your authenticity and shine brightly! Choose to be different and do the things you genuinely love and are good at. Decide to live life to the fullest and thrive rather than survive.

Use the knowledge that you have learned in this book as a stepping stone to learn more about these topics. Remember that knowledge truly is power. The more you invest in your future, the greater your rewards will be.

Life Owes You Nothing

While you might think they did, your parents did not always have it easy, and they had to learn and work hard to create the life they have. Your parents did their best and worked hard to prepare you for the real world. The rest is now up to you; make them proud and show them that you appreciate all they have done for you.

Life is a gift and owes you nothing. If you work hard and stay committed in all areas of your life, you can achieve your goals. Remember that nothing comes easily, and input equals output. Life is not always easy or fair; remember to always focus on the positive no matter what comes your way. Keep your eyes on the prize and be the very best you can be.

Be a person who thinks outside the box and uses the tools you have to thrive. Set achievable goals, invest in yourself, and explore the subjects that interest you. Whether academic, personal, or career-related, having goals gives you some extra direction and motivation.

Although you may face difficult times, complaining doesn't make things easier; it only wastes energy. Use your energy to find solutions and make positive changes. Don't be discouraged if failures or setbacks arise; instead, see obstacles as divine stepping stones to improve, learn and grow.

Thank You

Thank you so much for purchasing my book.

The marketplace is filled with dozens and dozens of other similar books but you took a chance and chose this one. And I hope it was well worth it.

So again, THANK YOU for getting this book and for making it all the way to the end.

Before you go, I wanted to ask you for one small favor.

Could you please consider posting a review for my book on the platform? Posting a review is the best and easiest way to support the work of independent authors like me.

Your feedback will help me to keep writing the kind of books that will help you get the results you want. It would mean a lot to me to hear from you.

REVIEW ON AMAZON US → 

REVIEW ON AMAZON UK → 

About The Author

Emily Carter is an author who loves helping teens with their biggest turn point in life, adulting. She grew up in New York and is happily married to her high school sweetheart. She also has two own children.

In her free time, Emily is an avid volunteer at a local food bank and enjoys hiking, traveling, and reading books on personal development. With over a decade of experience in the education and parenting field she has seen the difference that good parenting and the right tips can make in a teenager's life. She is now an aspiring writer through which she shares her insights and advice on raising happy, healthy, and resilient children, teens and young adults.

Emily's own struggles with navigating adulthood and overcoming obstacles inspired her to write. She noticed a gap in education regarding teaching essential life skills to teens and young adults, and decided to write comprehensive guides covering everything from money and time management to job searching and communication skills. Emily hopes her books will empower teens and young adults to live their best lives and reach their full potential.

To find more of her books, visit her Amazon Author page at:

https://www.amazon.com/author/emily-carter

References

A quote by Aristotle. (n.d.). Quotespedia. https://www.quotespedia.org/authors/a/aristotle/knowing-yourself-is-the-beginning-of-all-wisdom-aristotle/

A quote by Benjamin Franklin. (n.d.). GoodReads. https://www.goodreads.com/quotes/tag/money

A quote by Bret Morrison. (n.d.). A-Z Quotes. https://www.azquotes.com/quotes/topics/life-skills.html

A quote by E E Cummings. (n.d.). BrainyQuote. https://www.brainyquote.com/quotes/e_e_cummings_161593?src=t_teen

A quote by Friedrich Schiller. (n.d.). BrainyQuote. https://www.brainyquote.com/topics/teen-quotes

A quote by Nelson Mandela. (2019). BrainyQuote. https://www.brainyquote.com/quotes/nelson_mandela_157855

A quote by Robert Greene. (n.d.). Quote Fancy. https://quotefancy.com/skills-quotes

A quote by Russ Harris. (2022, March 18). PositivePsychology.com. https://positivepsychology.com/mental-health-quotes/

Made in the USA
Monee, IL
07 July 2026

56548201R00046